Anxiety Alchemy

HOW TO IMPROVE MENTAL HEALTH

WITH ANCIENT WISDOM

MIKE GUARNERI

Anxiety Alchemy:

How to Improve Mental Health with Ancient Wisdom

Published in the United States by Greenlamp, an imprint of Greenlamp LLC, Orange County, California

Greenlamp, LLC

30021 Tomas St., Suite 300

Rancho Santa Margarita, CA 92688

ISBN: 978-1-963977-04-2

To my wonderful wife. Her constant love, support, and encouragement were vital to the writing of this book.

Disclaimer

The system within this book is <u>not</u> a replacement for professional mental health treatments from a licensed professional. **I am <u>not</u> in any way a mental health professional.**

The system outlined is meant as a supplemental treatment. There is no guarantee whatsoever that you will experience any or a certain level of beneficial results from Anxiety Alchemy. I designed this system as a treatment for myself. I am sharing it with you in the hopes you will have the same beneficial results.

If you are experiencing any mental health challenges and have not sought the help of a licensed mental health practitioner, please do so immediately. This book is not your answer.

Table of Contents

Chapter One

How Did We Get Here?

About two years ago, I was suffering from anxiety and depression.

I was burnt out and miserable at my job. The only thing I got out of it was more anxiety and stress.

To make matters worse, we were still in the late stages of the COVID-19 pandemic.

I had nothing to look forward to, and life was bleak.

Even though the result was predictable, it still took me by surprise when it happened.

I suffered a mental breakdown!

Or, to be more precise, I suffered a severe panic attack one night.

It was the worst experience of my life. I thought I was going to die. No joke. I jolted out of bed in the middle of the night in a cold sweat, with my heart racing, my head pounding, and unable to breathe.

It had to be the end. What else could it be?

Well, fortunately, I wasn't dying. It turned out that it was the most severe panic attack I ever had. It took an entire week for me to settle back down to normal.

After a year, I concluded that mental health medications and talk therapy were not getting me to the good mental health I greatly desired. I decided that there were two things I wanted.

First, I wanted to be able to contribute to the treatment of my anxiety and depression. Secondly, I wanted to do this in a non-traditional, natural way.

But there was more to it than that.

I also really wanted to help other people suffering from anxiety and depression. And I wanted to do so in a way that could be utilized well into the future to provide people with more peace of mind.

My Journey

So, you may be wondering exactly how I got to this point. Well, after the previously mentioned mental breakdown, it was clear I needed professional help.

I tried mental health medications. There are tons of them. Finding the correct medication(s) and dosages is a trial-and-error process. It can take a long time.

Although mental health medications are important, don't forget about their side effects. They can be unpleasant. Believe it or not, one of the medications gave me tinnitus.

I tried talk therapy, and it was invaluable to me initially but became less so over time. The strategies provided to me were hit or miss.

Overall, it was clear to me that medications and/or talk therapy were not going to get me to the level of mental health I greatly desired.

So, my big question became: what non-traditional or alternative treatments might address the deficiencies left by traditional treatments?

I also became acutely aware that other anxiety and depression sufferers were also struggling to treat their mental health issues with traditional treatments.

But how was I supposed to help them, regardless of how much I wanted? I am just learning how to deal with my own mental health issues.

I am not a mental health professional nor an expert in alternative treatments. People will think I am crazy if I start pushing treatments out of the norm.

And most importantly, I am very uncomfortable putting myself out in public view. It causes me anxiety. Before I began this journey, I barely had any presence on the internet.

Meeting My Island Mentor

To be clear, this is not a mentor on an island but an island that is a mentor. Yes, it sounds crazy, but it's true.

I decided that I would venture on my own and see if I could somehow find a natural supplemental treatment for myself.

I took some time to determine if there was any particular place or time when I wasn't experiencing anxiety and depression and felt that I was in good mental health.

The answer came to me rather quickly. It was the time I spent in Ireland. But it had to be because I was on vacation and relaxed, or maybe just a coincidence. After all, what does an island have to do with mental health?

I determined there was nothing to pursue here and moved on.

My Dealer and My Therapist

It didn't take me long to realize that my traditional treatments were becoming as disruptive as the illnesses they were supposed to treat. They were promising more than they could deliver, and I was expecting more from them than I should have.

My psychiatrist was happy to keep doling out mental health drugs to me. It started to feel like I was participating in drug deals.

"Hey, Mike. I've got this new medication that is supposed to cure your anxiety and increase your IQ by 20 points. Let's give it a try. The worst thing that can happen is you lose your remaining hair, and your tongue turns black."

Obviously, this is an exaggeration for effect, but it really started to feel like this.

My therapist is great! I still use her to this day, even if it is less frequently. She immensely helped me when I needed it. But now, our talks feel more like catch-up sessions than actual therapy.

In hindsight, they both served me well and continue to serve me, but I do need to protect myself when their treatments become counterproductive.

Ireland Whispers in My Ear

Or, in reality, it hits me over the head with a pint of Guinness.

After a while, I became tired of playing the medication roulette wheel and was sick and tired of dealing with side effects.

To compound the situation, I wasn't having any luck with the strategies my therapist was giving me. It was easy for me to analyze them and how they were supposed to work. Knowing this information made them useless.

So, I returned to the exercise of where and when I was experiencing good mental health.

My answer was still Ireland. There had to be something about this small, wonderful island.

Next, I took a deep dive into Ireland to determine what had impacted me so much.

After a while, I realized it was the landscape. I am not talking about the mountains, lakes, and pastures. What I mean is the land and what it says—the energy it contains.

I learned that the ancient Irish were one with the land. They lived in harmony with it and shared energy or some sort of life force. However, I couldn't put my finger on it precisely.

I noticed that ancient Ireland is present in modern Ireland. The Island's history isn't necessarily nestled safely inside a museum; the Island is the history.

You cannot go far from any point on the Island without coming across a remnant or reminder of those ancient inhabitants. You just need to be observant.

I feel that the ancient ways and mindsets are still present in the people of Ireland today.

It became crystal clear to me that ancient wisdom holds answers for today's mental health questions.

A Grand Decision

I was reluctant to seek alternative treatment within ancient wisdom because I didn't want to waste my time in a possible never-ending black hole.

But, in light of traditional treatments failing to help me achieve my desired level of mental health, I was fed up. It was time to take matters into my own hands.

It was go time!

It was time to commit myself to researching, learning, and testing potential mental health treatments that ancient wisdom may hold.

The Long Winding Road

Despite having an abundance of research sources available, I didn't know how to develop the knowledge I obtained in my quest.

This put me in a negative place and caused me anxiety. I didn't have much experience in academic research or knowledge development. I knew I could do it but needed a logical and efficient system.

After a couple of months, I found it.

While researching knowledge development systems online, I discovered the ANTINET Zettelkasten. It was based on the work of a German sociologist named Nicolas Luhmann.

I contacted the ANTINET's creator and hired him to teach me the best and correct way to use his ANTINET for knowledge development.

Crisis averted...

Then, I was on a roll researching, learning, and developing knowledge.

Since ancient wisdom is quite a large area to cover, I decided to concentrate first on Ireland-related topics. That's what got me going, after all.

So, I started researching Celtic societies with an emphasis on Druidry.

Quickly, I ran into a significant problem. Comparatively, not much is known about the ancient Celts, and especially not the Druids. They were an oral society, so very little was written down.

Most of what we know about the Druids is from second and third-hand accounts from biased sources.

However, I realized I was not the only one who experienced this. There are people much smarter than I who have been researching, studying, and figuring things out for quite a while.

I immediately started contacting people whose perspectives I valued. I thought speaking to people such as Philip Carr-Gomm and Eimear Burke of the Order of Bards, Ovates, and Druids, a modern Druidry organization, would be invaluable. I also contacted Dara Molloy, Tiffany Lazic, Paraic Donoghue, and others.

I could not believe the reception I received from these fantastic people!

My very first interview was with Philip Carr-Gomm. If you are unfamiliar with Philip, he was the head of the Order of Bards, Ovates, and Druids for approximately thirty years, among other things, and is also a wonderful man.

I learned so much from these people, and they gave me so much hope. It was amazing that these esteemed people would give me the time of day and graciously share their time and knowledge. I will never forget it.

In the end, I discovered that, at least in the study and practice of ancient wisdom, people are very friendly and helpful. I stand ready and willing to return the favor. After this, I utilized various methods and perspectives to extract more knowledge than I thought was available.

With my newly found confidence, I researched the Celts and Druids, looking for those special practices that may provide supplemental relief to the symptoms of anxiety and depression.

I discovered that Catholic monks had adopted many Celtic practices, incorporating them as their own. The monks wrote down many of these practices and their sources.

This left me with a detailed list of Celtic practices and traditions. However, what to do with this list?

I researched each practice to determine if it was worth testing. After my research, I eliminated any practice that would not fit into our modern world or be deemed offensive.

Testing commenced with the practices remaining on my list. I developed procedures to enact them and recorded the results.

It became clear there were Celtic practices that improved my anxiety and depression. To this day, I still perform some of these.

Along the way, I shared my insights and results via YouTube and an online newsletter. This culminated with my e-book, *"Ten Celtic Practices to Level Up Your Mind and Relieve Anxiety and Depression."*

"The Great New Thing"

After experiencing all of these challenges, I realized a few things:

- It is possible for me to use ancient wisdom in treatments for modern mental health issues.
- I can add value to the lives of my fellow anxiety and depression sufferers by sharing my results.
- Good mental health treatments are not limited to the standard of medications and talk therapy.

To recap, since I initiated my quest for good mental health through ancient wisdom, I discovered:

- the sophisticated knowledge development system called the ANTINET, which would become the hub of my research.
- that there are a plethora of friendly people who are happy to share their time and knowledge graciously.
- based on my positive results with Celtic practices, ancient wisdom can definitely be a source for supplemental mental health treatments.

I was unsure what to call my work. Ultimately, I decided on:

Anxiety Alchemy

Indeed, this name doesn't encapsulate ancient wisdom in its entirety, but it alludes to it. The name is also exciting. It teases the uniqueness and possibilities of using ancient wisdom for modern mental health.

Subsequently, I devised a two-fold master plan:

- Share the success of my Celtic practices with the world, hoping that people would potentially benefit from them. I would do this via YouTube videos, my electronic newsletter, and my e-book, *"10 Celtic Practices to Level Up Your Mind and Relieve Anxiety and Depression."*
- Continue to research and develop my knowledge in the search for more ancient wisdom to support mental health.

But then I was thrown for an unexpected loop.

The Celtic practices didn't spread like I had hoped. The reactions I received were more quality than quantity. I was very frustrated because I knew they could help people.

Secondly, my research had run dry. There seemed nothing more for me to find in the world of the ancient Celts and Druids. And since the other categories of ancient wisdom were so wide-sweeping, I didn't know what to do next, if anything.

The Deep Dark Hole

There I was, in my bed at 4:30 pm on a Friday afternoon. I was engulfed in complete darkness as I stared up at the ceiling.

Suddenly, my wife entered the room and turned on the overhead lights, not realizing I was there. She asked if I was alright. I lied and said yes so she wouldn't worry.

In reality, I was having a relapse of my mental health issues. I was depressed with my current situation and was experiencing anxiety about what to do next.
It had been a year since I quit my full-time accounting job to pursue helping others and myself with alternative mental health treatments.

It was the first time I had set off independently, seemingly failing. I was stuck at this point, experiencing my worst mental health since my breakdown. I spent a few months in this rut.

What to do next?

Be miserable forever by crawling back to the world of financial services? I had now experienced freedom from it, so the thought of going back only made me more depressed.

Should I stay the course or give up?

Then, one day, I spoke to my friend Scott, who introduced me to his ANTINET. He told me about a new project he would launch in a month or so. It was a top-shelf writing incubator.

It sounded so great that it re-enlivened me.

But what would I research and write about? My endeavor to improve mental well-being through ancient wisdom hit a roadblock.

However, at the time, I was rediscovering history and falling in love with it again. It reconfirmed that I was on the right track before I let myself become overwhelmed and stuck in a rut. I didn't adapt like I should have.

I realized that the best way forward was to pick the area of ancient wisdom that most interested me, utilize what I could from it, and then move on to the next area of interest.

So, I did just that and decided to focus on the ancient wisdom of the Occult. Yes, I know that some occult practices and organizations are not ancient, but it is where their knowledge base is sourced.

Moving Forward

Reinvigorated, I started researching different areas of the Occult and had a great time doing so. Finally, different pieces started to come together in a beautiful tapestry. The connections and discoveries gave me boundless passion.

A Great New Adventure

Buoyed by recent achievements, I embarked on a quest to uncover ancient insights that could guide me toward optimal mental wellness. This endeavor spurred me to develop and experiment with a personalized system inspired by these timeless principles.

This new strategy has been successful for me so far. The book you are now reading is a culmination of this success. I will continue down this path.

Results

- I experienced the positive impact of using ancient wisdom for better mental health.
- I created my first system using ancient wisdom to help people suffering from anxiety (The Anxiety Alchemy System).
- In six months, I went from despair and being ready to give up to being reinvigorated and producing the book now in your hands.
- Many people have expressed gratitude for my efforts and shared how profoundly it helped them, particularly during challenging periods.

Through this book, I hope many people experience the positive mental health benefits of **the Anxiety Alchemy System.**

Who is this Guy?

As I spring to life anew, having reinvented myself, I have started calling myself "**the Anxiety Alchemy Guy.**"

People seem to like it, and so do I.

So mote it be...

In Summary

As you may recall, I wanted to be able to better participate in my anxiety and depression treatments. I have achieved this thanks to Celtic Practices and the Anxiety Alchemy System.

I also wanted to find non-traditional ways of treating the symptoms of anxiety and depression. This was found through ancient wisdom.

But more important than my System and books is the fact that I have been able to help my fellow anxiety and depression sufferers.

If my work helps people improve their mental health and peace of mind, I will consider it a great success.

My Transformation

In just a short period of time, I had gone from a state of severe anxiety and depression to creating something that helps others by providing them with alternative mental health treatments based on ancient wisdom.

I am the Anxiety Alchemy Guy!

And while having a positive impact on my mental health is nice, I got what I really wanted.

That is to help you achieve good mental health.

All this is thanks to ancient wisdom, specifically the **Anxiety Alchemy System.**

CHAPTER TWO

Erin's Story

"Bing bong!"

The train doors opened. Erin rushed into the train car, did a quick scan, and bee-lined to an available seat like a guided missile.

As Erin sat there, her heart raced, she breathed hard, and she broke out in a cold sweat.

Across the aisle from her was her friend Larry. She met Larry on the train home one day, and they became friends. Larry is her commuting buddy and source of support.

Larry asked, "Erin, are you ok?"

Larry knew she wasn't, but he also knew the best thing he could do for her was keep an eye on her and be supportive.

He learned previously that the worst thing is to say, "Calm down" or "Relax." These two phrases tend to make people suffering from an anxiety attack worse.

So, yes, Erin suffers from extreme anxiety.

And that is **EXTREME ANXIETY!**

Despite her mental health medications and her talk therapy, she still has anxiety attacks about going to work. It's not the work itself that is the source of Erin's anxiety. *It is the commute to work.*

From the moment she wakes up in the morning on a work day, Erin experiences anxiety. It is also awful on Sunday nights, while she anticipates the commute the following day.

Erin works for a lovely company in New York City but lives in the suburbs. To get to work, she must drive to the train station, take the train into New York City, and then take the subway to her office.

This whole process causes her so much anxiety that it overcomes her anti-anxiety medications and talk therapy. Erin is so frustrated and tired of this being a problem every workday. After all, she is only twenty-four years old and has her whole career ahead of her.

Fortunately for Erin, she is on vacation next week. It will be a nice break from the commute, but it won't be an easy week.

You see, she recently picked up a new book about using the ancient wisdom of alchemy to combat anxiety (this book). Erin plans to implement the Anxiety Alchemy System. It is easy to understand, but she knows confronting the demons of her anxiety will be difficult!

Erin's story to be continued...

CHAPTER THREE

Anxiety

Anxiety is a mental health disease. There are numerous flavors and severities. Anxiety can be temporary, caused by the environment or a particular situation. Or it can be a clinical diagnosis caused by genetics.

The most common mental disorders in the world are anxiety disorders, impacting 301 million people worldwide in 2019. That is 4% of the global population.[1] These statistics do not take into account the number of unreported anxiety sufferers.

Some of the more common types of anxiety disorders are Generalized Anxiety Disorder, Social Anxiety Disorder, and Panic Disorder.

The gold standard treatments for anxiety disorders are anti-anxiety medications and talk therapy. However, individually or combined, they may not fully address your anxiety issues. I have experienced this personally.

The problem with medications and talk therapy is that it may take some time to realize the full benefits of the treatment.

---

[1] *"Anxiety Disorders."* World Health Organization, June 8, 2022. https://www.who.int/news-room/fact-sheets/detail/mental-disorders.

Even though medications, in theory, should have a quick effect, finding the correct medications and dosages may take time and trial and error.

It took me a whole year to do so.

Mental health medications also come with unwanted side effects.

Regarding talk therapy, I found it took a good ten sessions to derive a helpful benefit. Shortly after that, I found it to have quickly declining returns. There are always variables, such as your connection with the therapist and what kind of talk therapy you use.

Where **Anxiety Alchemy** comes into the picture is when mental health medications and/or talk therapy are not fully resolving your anxiety and getting you to your desired level of mental health. I believe this is the point at which it is time for you to consider alternative supplemental treatments.

What I recommend against is adding even more medications to your treatment regime. For example, there are medications on the market whose purpose is to treat depression when there is only a partial response to the original depression medication.

We can't throw more and more pills at our mental health issues. Medications help, but there are other ways.

Natural ways. Ancient ways.

CHAPTER FOUR

Alchemy

What was made from a single piece of emerald or green crystal?

What contains a very powerful, multi-layered message of hidden meanings and a process to reach enlightened spirituality?

If you answered the *"Emerald Tablet,"* you are correct!

"The Emerald Tablet offers each one of us the chance not only to directly participate in the quantum leap of consciousness that can safely lead us into the third millennium, but also to do so as a real person true to ourselves and in accordance with the Soul of the Universe.[2]"

Ancient Egyptians believed the Emerald Tablet was a divine document with many layers of meaning and possible interpretations. Thus, it was not easy to understand and peel away the layers. The Emerald Tablet covers numerous topics within the layers of

---

[2] Hauck, Dennis William. *The Emerald Tablet: Alchemy for Personal Transformation* New York, Penguin/Arkana, 1999. Introduction, para. 7.

understanding. Among them are science, psychology, religion, spirituality, and physiology.

A likeness of the Emerald Tablet.

The Emerald tablet is thought to have been authored by the Egyptian god Thoth, also known as Hermes Trismegistus. Whether he was a god, a legend, a natural person, or a set of ideas and principles is debated.

The Emerald Tablet, among other interpretations, lays out the steps of the Alchemical process, the basics of Hermetic philosophy, and the correspondences between above and below.

It was translated around 330 BCE by Alexandrian scholars.[3]

Let's take a look at a translation.

The Emerald Tablet[4]

"In truth without deceit, certain and most veritable.

That which is Below corresponds to that which is Above, and that which is Above corresponds to that which is Below, to accomplish the miracles of the One Thing, through the meditation of the One Mind, so do all created things originate from this One Thing, through transformation.

Its father is the Sun; its mother the Moon. The Wind carries it in its belly; its nurse is the Earth. It is the origin of All, the consecration of the Universe; its inherent strength is perfected, if it is turned to Earth.

Separate the Earth from the Fire, the Subtle from the Gross, gently and with great ingenuity. It rises from the

---

[3] Hauck, Dennis William. *The Emerald Tablet: Alchemy for Personal Transformation*. New York, Penguin/Arkana, 1999. Introduction, para. 2.

[4] Hauck, Dennis William. *The Emerald Tablet: Alchemy for Personal Transformation*. New York, Penguin/Arkana, 1999. Chapter 3.

Earth to heaven and descends again to Earth, thereby combining within itself the powers of both the Above and Below.

Thus will you obtain the Glory of the whole Universe. All obscurity will be clear to you. This is the greatest Force of all Powers, because it overcomes every subtle thing and penetrates every solid thing.

In this way the Universe is created. From this comes many wonderous applications, because this is the pattern.

Therefore, am I called Thrice Greatest Hermes, having all three parts of the Wisdom of the whole Universe, herein have I completely explained the Operation of the Sun."

[End Emerald Tablet]

So, what do you think?

How does the text of the Emerald Tablet relate to Alchemy? Alchemists determined the operations for the alchemical process are contained within the Emerald Tablet, whether you seek to turn lead into gold or turn your materialistic soul into an enlightened spirituality.

Incidentally, during my research, I stumbled upon an intriguing nugget of trivia - pun fully intended. In the heyday of alchemy during the Renaissance, alchemists regarded anything with a golden hue as genuine gold.

Here are the seven alchemical operations as per the Emerald Tablet:

Calcination
Dissolution
Separation
Conjunction
Fermentation
Distillation
Coagulation

These operations can be executed physically, spiritually, or both. I will discuss each operation and show you how it is a part of the Anxiety Alchemy System (AAS).

Chapter Five

How To Use Anxiety Alchemy

The following seven chapters will take you through the operations of Alchemy. For each operation, I will very briefly describe the physical process. That will be followed by a detailed explanation of my Anxiety Alchemy System (AAS). Lastly, each Chapter will conclude with the continuation of "Erin's Story" for illustrative purposes.

It is very important not to read and implement the stages out of order. Alchemy is a specific process that needs to be performed in order.

The Anxiety Alchemy System is different in that it targets specific anxiety issues, as opposed to being a generalized system for better mental health. To be clear, the purpose of this system is to identify and resolve a specific persistent anxiety, not to reduce anxiety in general.

You may implement AAS as often as you wish for different specific anxieties. **Do not repeat the process for any given anxiety unless directed in Chapter Twelve.**

Before we get into the nitty gritty of Calcination, the first operation, I would like to give you some advice.

According to Brian Cotnoir, author of numerous alchemy books, we should be aware of the "Four Rules of Action" while undergoing an alchemical process.

The Four Rules of Action[5]

Rule #1- Actions have results:
Every action has a result. They may be unintended, but there are results.

Rule #2 - Results have causes:
If there is a result, there must have been an action that gave rise to it.

Rule #3 - Like Comes from like:
Oak trees come from acorns, and tigers come from tigers. Maple trees do not produce goats, and chickens don't give birth to vacuum cleaners.

Rule #4 - Actions grow and expand:
Once an action has started, it continues to ripple outward.

Keep these rules in mind as you use the Anxiety Alchemy System. It is a system of action. Every stage of the process involves participation. You don't experience alchemy sitting on the couch watching Netflix.

---

[5] Cotnoir, Brian. *On Alchemy: Essential Practices and Making Art as Alchemy.* New York, Watkins Media, 2023. Chap. Essential Practices, paras. 20-23.

Chapter Six

Calcination

"The first of the seven operations of alchemy is Calcination, the heating and pulverization of a solid to drive off water and other volatile compounds.[6]"

Physical

Alchemists believed that they could turn prima materia into gold using the process of alchemy.

In the first operation, Calcination, the alchemist completely burns up the prima materia under extremely high heat until it turns into white ash. Metals can be reduced to white ash if a calcinating agent is applied. For example, if sulfur is added, lead can be burned to white ash.

---

[6] Hauck, Dennis William. *The Emerald Tablet: Alchemy for Personal Transformation*. New York, Penguin/Arkana, 1999. Chap. 11, para 1.

Anxiety Alchemy System

The Anxiety Alchemy System addresses specific, persistent anxieties on a case-by-case basis. Once you have selected the anxiety you wish to address, you are ready to begin AAS.

The Process

Step 1 - This is the operation of emotions. It is time to let your anxiety-driven emotions out in a controlled way. Get comfortable in your favorite meditation position. Be sure that you have paper and a writing implement nearby.

Step 2—We start calcination by heating ourselves mentally. Remember, Calcination requires extreme heat, so we are, in effect, preheating the oven. We will use a meditation called "Bellows Breath" to do this.

Bellows Breath[7]

" In this exercise, the alchemist sits cross-legged on the floor and tries to focus his energy at the navel or birth point. The breath is very rapid, continuous and powerful with no pause between inhaling and exhaling. The rate is about two exhalations per second. As he exhales, he pushes out the air like a bellows by pulling the navel

---

[7] Hauck, Dennis William. *The Emerald Tablet: Alchemy for Personal Transformation.* New York, Penguin/Arkana, 1999. Chap. 11, Cauldron of the Metals, para. 2.

point in toward the spine. When he inhales, he uses a forward thrust of the navel to bring air into the lungs. He tries to keep a smooth, balanced breath with no emphasis on either the taking in or expulsion of air. After a few minutes of "fanning the fire," he starts to feel a warmth rise from the stomach and accumulate in the head."

It should take you about five minutes for this meditation to get you warmed up.

Step 3—Now that we are warmed up, it is time to unleash our anxiety-related emotions. We will do this by doing a meditation called "Roasting Cinnabar."

During this meditation, you need to focus on your rage, anger, and frustration towards your anxiety. Get mad! Think about all the harmful components that contribute to this anxiety.

Burn That Damn Anxiety to the Ground!

This will be emotionally painful, but I am 100% confident you can do it.

You took the step of committing yourself to trying out my non-mainstream Anxiety Alchemy System. If you can do that in the face of anxiety, you have what it takes to feel and process all your negative anxiety-related emotions and thoughts.

And don't worry; this is the only super intense operation of the System.

To the Roasting Cinnabar Meditation.

Roasting Cinnabar[8]

" Start out sitting in a comfortable chair or lying propped up by cushions on a bed or couch. Slowly count back from ten, and with each count, take a slower and fuller breath while progressively relaxing every part of the body—starting with the toes and working up to the scalp muscles. Then try to visualize the bright red cinnabar roasting over a blazing fire,..."

I have adjusted the remaining part of the meditation to adapt it to the Anxiety Alchemy System.

It is as follows:

Feel yourself moving towards the fire's heat. As you approach it, your body starts feeling warm, hot, and then blazing hot.

You can barely stand staying in the meditation. The only way to do so is to distract yourself from the burning. You do so by generating intense rage about your anxiety. You break the anxiety up into its component parts, the smaller things that make up your "Anxiety." After you

---

[8] Hauck, Dennis William. *The Emerald Tablet: Alchemy for Personal Transformation*. New York, Penguin/Arkana, 1999. Chap. 11, Roasting Cinnabar, para. 5.

note them, throw them into the fire, watch them undergo calcification, and burn to white ash.

The meditation is now complete.

Before you run to get a cold drink to cool down, write down the component parts of the anxiety you calcinated in your meditation.

Make sure you don't skip the writing part of this operation. You will need it later on.

Step 4 - Now, the Anxiety Alchemist will symbolically calcinate the anxiety's component parts by burning them to ash.

Ensure that there are two copies of the components. It doesn't matter if they are written in a notebook, on scraps of paper, or on index cards; it's all the same.

The Alchemist may say a few words before performing a ceremonial calcination, and a small private ritual may also be performed.

Then, the Anxiety Alchemist burns them up.

Fire safety should be the Alchemist's number one concern. I take no responsibility for any fire damage.

During Anxiety Alchemy Calcination, the Alchemist has taken their anxiety out of their body and burned it to white ash, along with the related emotions caused by the anxiety.

Until the Conjunction operation, the Alchemist will view their anxiety as just a thing. They will have no feelings. They will be logical and analytical.

Completing the Calcination operation is a giant success. Congratulations!

Example

We will use our friend Erin from Chapter Two as an example throughout the Anxiety Alchemy operations.

If you remember, Erin is extremely anxious about commuting to work in New York City. This anxiety is impacting her both physically and emotionally.

Erin is ready for the calcination of her commuting anxiety.

Step 1: She is all set in her favorite recliner, with a pen and scraps of paper beside her.

Step 2 - Erin performs the "Bellows Breath" meditation and gets warmed up.

Step 3 – Then, she performs the "Roasting Cinnabar" meditation and rages against her anxiety. She lets out all her feelings about her commuting anxiety and how it has impacted her. One by one, she thinks about the component parts of her anxiety and throws them into the fire. They will soon become white ash.

Erin then writes down on little scraps of paper the anxiety component parts that she calcinated in her meditation.

Her list is as follows:

- Worry about having an anxious stomachache before leaving the house.

- Worry about being late for the train.

- Worry about not getting a parking spot.

- Worry about not standing where the train doors open.

- Worry about not getting a seat on the train.

- Worry about the train being late.

- Worry about there being too many people at Penn Station.

- Worry about the subway running on time.

- Worry of the New York City crime.

- Worry that I will get to work late.

- Worry that everybody will be disappointed in me if I am late.

That's some list; no wonder Erin has anxiety about commuting to work.

Now, Erin does the most important thing. She follows the Anxiety Alchemy Guy's instructions and makes duplicate copies of her scraps of paper.

Step 4 - Erin now goes outside to her backyard. She has a sarcastic fake funeral for the components of her anxiety.

Out comes a lighter, and the components are reduced to ash.

Erin congratulates herself and returns to celebrate the successful calcination of her commuting-related anxiety.

Chapter Seven

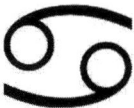

Dissolution

The second operation of the Alchemical process is Dissolution.

Physical

At the end of the Calcination operation, the alchemist was left with scorched matter in the form of a white powder.

Now, the alchemist adds water (or sometimes a solvent) to the white powder and heats it over a low, steady flame. Eventually, when all that will dissolve has dissolved, the Alchemist will be left with the component pieces.

Without the dissolution step being appropriately done, the alchemist will compromise the whole alchemical process.

Anxiety Alchemy System

In the previous operation, the Anxiety Alchemist burned their anxiety to the ground. In the process, they also burned off their emotions. They can now look at their anxiety in a detached manner as if it is something separate from them that they are trying to fix.

Look at it as though the Alchemist is a mechanic, and their pile of white anxiety powder is the car they are working on.

Step 1 - It is now time for the Anxiety Alchemist to dissolve the white powder of their anxiety in water. What remains will be the components of their anxiety, both good and bad. Their burnt thoughts and emotions will dissolve into the water and no longer be a factor in their alchemical process.

Step 2 - Perform the "Bain Marie" meditation. Maria Prophetissa supposedly invented this meditation. According to legend, Maria was Moses' sister.

Bain Marie Meditation[9]

"Here is how it works: Seated or lying down, calm yourself with several deep breaths, and then inhale very slowly. Imagine you are taking in the warm, dissolving waters of the Bain Marie. Hold the breath for a few seconds and let it "work" on those painful emotions or

---

[9] Hauck, Dennis William. *The Emerald Tablet: Alchemy for Personal Transformation.* New York, Penguin/Arkana, 1999. Chap. 12, Dissolving Meditations, para. 1.

on any area in your mind or body where you feel tension or pain. Then exhale slowly and deeply—as deeply as you can—and imagine those hardened hurtful areas melting away. Repeat this circulation of dissolving "waters" as long as it takes until you feel genuine relief. Then relax and breathe normally. If you feel the troublesome areas returning, begin the Bain Marie again. Remarkable results can be obtained with this very basic exercise in just a few sessions."

All those feelings and emotions you burned during calcination must be entirely dissolved. We want them gone. As the meditation indicates, repeat it until you no longer feel those anxious feelings and emotions.

Example

Step 1 - Erin contemplates the operation of dissolution and the thought of the continued breakdown of her commuting to work anxiety.

Step 2 - Erin is getting into the flow of the Anxiety Alchemy System and feeling its effects, so she decides to one-up Mike and do the Bain Marie meditation in a nice warm bath.

Why didn't I think of that before and include it in my book? Hang on, I guess I just did.

Chapter Eight

Separation

The third operation of the alchemical process is Separation.

Physical

During this operation, the alchemist will isolate and extract any remaining material from the alchemical solution created during the Dissolution operation. This will be accomplished through further heating, sifting, and filtration.

Anxiety Alchemy System

In this operation, the Anxiety Alchemist sifts through the remaining material in the alchemical solution.

Step 1 - There are a bunch of harmful anxiety component materials in the alchemical solution.

The Alchemist needs to sift those out. **They are done fueling this anxiety.** They have been burnt to ashes, drowned, and had all emotions disconnected from them.

If you remember, these are the components from Chapter Six—Calcination—the ones I requested the Alchemist duplicate.

Step 2 - Now, the Alchemist is going to take the harmful components of the anxiety and symbolically drown them.

You may do this however you like. My favorite way is to flush them down the toilet. I get to drown them and wave goodbye to them.

Disclaimer: **Please note that if harmful components are flushed down the toilet, I am not responsible for any plumbing issues that may arise.**

Step 3—Our Alchemist is not done separating. They look at their alchemical solution. There are bright and glowing things. These are the good things that were suppressed by the anxiety—the things that their anxiety took hostage. Well, they will be back and better than ever.

Pull the "good things" out of the alchemical solution by writing them on scraps of paper or similar material. Take your time with this. If given a chance, there is probably more good than expected.

The Anxiety Alchemist may wish to put a few of their favorites somewhere visible in a room they frequent. For example, I have mine on my desk, hanging off the bottom of my computer monitor.

Step 4 - Perform the "Alchemistic Aeration Meditation" a few times. Good on them if the Alchemist wishes to take up the challenge in the meditation.

Alchemistic Aeration Meditation[10]

"To try this yourself, sit upright in a chair and relax.

Using the diaphragm, take a deep breath while expanding the stomach. This is followed by a slow expansion of the rib cavity, culminating in upper lung breathing that can be felt all the way into the throat.

Then, exhale completely, starting at the base of the lungs and climaxing at the top. Exhalation should take twice as long as inhalation.

Practice inhaling for a count of eight and exhaling for a count of sixteen, while concentrating on filling and emptying all three levels of the lungs.

At first, it may not be easy to break years of improper breathing habits, but keep practicing until you are able to achieve these minimum periods of inhalation, retention, and exhalation.

––––––––––––––––––––

[10] Hauck, Dennis William. *The Emerald Tablet: Alchemy for Personal Transformation.* New York, Penguin/Arkana, 1999. Chap. 13, Alchemistic Aeration, para. 4.

They can be expanded in the proportion of three counts while holding the breath and two counts of exhalation for every one count of inhalation."

The Anxiety Alchemist's purpose in doing this meditation is twofold:

- To experience the freedom of deep breathing without the persistent impact of anxiety.

- To open their hearts and emotions for the next alchemical operation, Conjunction.

Example

Steps 1 and 2—Erin flushes the scraps of paper with her harmful anxiety components down the toilet. But once again, she must one-up the author and creator of the Anxiety Alchemy System. Erin tosses the scraps into the toilet by lighting them on fire, throwing them in, and flushing them.

Again, why am I just thinking of this now? It's pretty awesome, a Viking Funeral for anxiety.

To remind you, here is Erin's list of harmful anxiety components that she sent to Valhalla.

- Worry about having an anxious stomachache before leaving the house.

- Worry about being late for the train.

- Worry about not getting a seat on the train.

- Worry about not getting a parking spot.

- Worry about not standing where the train doors open.

- Worry about the train being late.

- Worry about there being too many people at Penn Station.

- Worry about the subway running on time.

- Worry of the New York City crime.

- Worry that I will get to work late.

- Worry that everybody will be disappointed in me if I am late.

Step 3 – Erin sits down to brainstorm good things that her anxiety had taken hostage but has now been freed in the alchemical solution.

Here is Erin's list:

- I can meet my friends for lunch or after work for drinks or dinner.

- My favorite gourmet coffee shop is right next to my office.

- I can have some real me time on the train to sleep, read, and listen to podcasts. No anxiety will interrupt me.

- I can make new friends on the train.

- My favorite clothing stores are in Manhattan.

- I can now pursue a relationship with a cute coworker who constantly flirts with me.

- I can again enjoy my job without showing up to work a wreck.

- I can run after work and train for the New York City Marathon.

Erin's anxiety deprived her of these things and probably many more.

She feels fantastic seeing the positive side of the commute.

Step 4 - Erin performs the Alchemistic Aeration Meditation and commits to doing it daily to reach its goal. It will definitely help her lung capacity during her marathon preparations.

Chapter Nine

Conjunction

The fourth operation of the alchemical process is Conjunction. During Conjunction, the unrefined goodness resulting from Separation is combined.

Physical

The alchemist takes his unrefined treasure and combines it, usually with the help of other chemical substances to help it bind.

The result is a very unstable object called the Lesser Stone.

Anxiety Alchemy System

Like the physical alchemist, the Anxiety Alchemist must combine all the goodness extracted during the Separation operation.

The Alchemist's creation will not hold without something else added as a binding agent.

Step 1 - The good parts of the Anxiety extracted in the Separation operation are reviewed for completeness and actual tangible value.

Step 2 - This is the most crucial step of Conjunction - the secret ingredient, the binding agent of all binding agents. It needs to be added to the Anxiety Alchemist's mixture.

This is the time when the Anxiety Alchemist adds their emotions back.

Do you remember in Chapter Six, Calcination, the Alchemist removed all emotions from their anxiety work? Then, they worked on it in a straightforward, logical, and arms-length manner during Dissolution and Separation.

Now, they add the emotions back into the mixture of only good anxiety material. How this is done is left to the Alchemist.

Step 3 - The last step of this operation is to perform an Earth meditation. The Alchemical Operation of Conjunction corresponds with the Earth.

Although I find this meditation helpful, it does require some advanced preparation and is not a vital part of the Anxiety Alchemy System. The Alchemist has the option of performing it or not.

An Earth Meditation[11]

"In a field or forest clearing, find a central location and mark it within a circle of rocks or use a natural marker such as a tree stump or boulder. Sit within the circle or near the landmark and face north.

Now, relax and contemplate each of the four directions as manifestations of the four elements both within you and in nature.

Spend ten minutes or so reflecting on the following qualities of each direction and then turn clockwise to face the next direction.

The object is to make the like elements resonate between you and nature.

First, look to the north. According to traditional Native American myth, the north, or polar, direction is associated with the Earth element. It is home to the powers of the Below: night, winter, the hidden sun, the fallen moon, ancestors, ancient wisdom, and unconditional love. It is also home to sacred horned animals, such as the reindeer and the white buffalo, or fantasy creatures like the unicorn. Try to actually feel the archetypal Earth, the dark powers of matter and the planet, as well as what it would be like to be a horned animal surviving in this untamed environment.

---

[11] Hauck, Dennis William. *The Emerald Tablet: Alchemy for Personal Transformation.* New York, Penguin/Arkana, 1999. Chapter 14, Working with Earth, paras. 5 - 9.

Next, turn eastward in the direction of the Air element. It is home to the rising sun, spring, birth, thought, synchronicity, and new beginnings. Out of the golden sky of the east comes the soaring eagle. Try to feel the optimism of the dawn and the freedom and perspective of the eagle. Listen closely to the Wind.

Then, turn to the south or equatorial direction, home of the Fire element. This is the direction of the noon sun, summer, childhood, passion, trust, and healing. The archetypes of the noontime sun are embodied in animal totems that include family or den-oriented animals like wolves, coyotes, and mountain lions, as well as domesticated animals like dogs and cats. Reexperience the warmth of the home fires and the innocence of childhood as you face the source of Fire.

Now turn to face the west, home of the Water element. Since the moon appears brightest after the setting of the sun, native cultures connect the lunar presence with the west. The western horizon is the direction of the sunset, Fall, maturity, harmony, introspection, deep feelings, and building confidence through meditation. Its totems are ocean-born mammals such as the dolphin and whale or hibernating animals like bears. Try to be especially still while looking west and open yourself to its unconscious, intuitive wisdom. Pay close attention to any signs of Water in the environment.

Finally, return to the north-facing position, but this time, try to feel all the varied energies of the different directions at once. Let them come together within you.

This is not a thinking process, so you have to open yourself up and let the elements flow into you and harmonize with the like elements within you.

Like our planet itself, you too are made up of Earth, Air, Fire, and Water. Like the planet, you too are alive with yet a fifth element. This is the central spot you created on the earth, the one point within you where all of the four elements come together to create the Quintessence, the one living person that you really are.

From this position, you can access the powers of the imaginal and spiritual realms in the Above and return to the Earth and matter in the Below, now able to perceive spirit in all things."

It is essential to note that the result of the Anxiety Alchemy System is similar to physical alchemy.

At the end of the Conjunction operation, a very fragile lesser stone of the Alchemist's anxiety will remain.

Take care not to let any harmful anxiety components creep back in during such a vulnerable state.

Example

Step 1 - Erin reviews the list of good things she extracted from her major anxiety. She determines it is complete enough. It has all the big ticket items. She could go on and on if she wanted to.

Step 2 - Erin slowly and deliberately mixes each element of anxiety goodness with her emotions. She does this by going one by one and thinking about the feeling each gives her. Erin not only wants to experience the feeling of thinking about it, she wants to feel it in action.

Erin, therefore, decides that she will visualize herself doing or experiencing each piece of goodness that was extracted from her anxiety.

For example, Erin closes her eyes and visualizes going out for drinks with friends after work. She goes through the steps in her head to experience them on some level.

Step 3 - Erin thinks the Earth meditation looks pretty good, so she decides to try it over the weekend in a local park.

At the end of the Conjunction operation, Erin has an unstable vessel that once carried the harmful components of her anxiety. However, it is now filled with the goodness she freed from her commuting anxiety.

Chapter Ten

Fermentation

The fifth operation of the Alchemical process is Fermentation.

Fermentation is the conversion of organic substances into new material using fermenting bacteria.

There are two parts to Fermentation:

Putrification: The process of the Lesser Stone rotting and decaying.

Fermentation: The rebirth of the dead and decaying matter.

Physical

The alchemist will apply heat and moisture to the lesser stone to start the process of Putrification. Remember from Chapter Nine that the Lesser Stone is very unstable and has a very short life expectancy in its current form.

Once Putrification is almost done, when there is a milky light fluid, the Alchemist may add other compounds to the Lesser Stone to aid it in its fermentation process.

This is just like adding yeast during alcohol fermentation. In its simplest form, yeast is added to crushed grapes to create wine.

But what just really happened in the wine fermentation example?

The crushed grapes were turned into a completely new substance, wine, during fermentation.

In alchemy, when one substance is turned into a completely new substance, it is called **transmutation**. So, in a nutshell, the full fermentation process is the death of the Lesser Stone and its rebirth into a new substance that will become the Philosopher's Stone—gold.

The alchemist will know when the fermentation process is complete when there is a thick yellow-flowing wax-like fluid.

Anxiety Alchemy System

The Anxiety Alchemist will undertake a similar but slightly modified process of Fermentation.

At the end of Chapter Nine, the Anxiety Alchemist had a Lesser Stone, an unstable anxiety shell containing the good qualities of commuting to work and good emotions and feelings.

Our Alchemist will transmute this Lesser Stone into a new, strong, stable vessel with the same contents through the full fermentation process.

The future Philosopher's Stone of the commuting anxiety.

For the Lesser Stone to be putrified, the Anxiety Alchemist must pick away at the Lesser Stone's shell, which is the anxiety shell.

Step 1 - Commit the list of goodness inside the anxiety shell to memory.

Step 2 - This second step needs to be done daily for at least a week, but no longer than it takes the Anxiety Alchemist to rot away the anxiety shell fully.

Step 2A - Each day, speak out loud the goodness list three times. This should be done from memory. When the Anxiety Alchemist does so, they should do it with deliberation and sincerity. When each item is said, the Alchemist should experience a shot of well-being.

Step 2B - During the Anxiety Alchemist's putrification period, they must be penalized for every time a thought of a negative aspect comes to mind.

The Alchemist will choose their penalty. This is just plain old behavior modification. It also helps the alchemist focus on not letting those thoughts creep in.

Step 3 - Now, the Anxiety Alchemist will add something to the process to help the putrified remains of their Lesser Stone ferment into their future Philosopher's Stone.

Whereas physical alchemy adds a fermenting substance as an aid, the Anxiety Alchemist will instead put the putrified material into a new strong vessel to be fermented.

This new strong vessel is the Anxiety Alchemist!

They will take their rotted material and integrate it back into themself.

How this is done is left to the discretion of the Anxiety Alchemist.

Recommended methods include:

- Meditating on the goodness that is now re-integrated into the person.

- Repeating an affirmation regarding the particular anxiety no longer being a part of the Anxiety Alchemist.

Example

Step 1 - Erin commits her list of goodness to memory.

Step 2:

2a - She deliberately repeats the list out loud before each of her three daily meals.

2B - Erin chooses a penalty of a fifteen-minute social media ban for each time she thinks of a negative aspect of her commuting anxiety.

Step 3 - Erin decides to employ the two methods recommended by Mike, the Anxiety Alchemy Guy.

Each day, she will carve out time for an extra ten-minute meditation to focus on the feelings of the reintegration of goodness into her body.

Erin also writes an affirmation, which she reads at least once daily.

Her affirmation is as follows:

I no longer have anxiety about commuting to work.

I have processed and removed all the harmful components that composed my anxiety.

I have discovered the beautiful aspects of commuting that were suppressed by my anxiety.

I have transmuted my anxiety into goodness.

I will now have wonderful commutes to work.

Erin now recognizes she is the new vessel and contains the future Philosopher's Stone of her commuting anxiety.

Chapter Eleven

Distillation

The sixth operation of alchemy is Distillation.

The purpose of Distillation is to take the new matter created during Fermentation and further refine and concentrate it. This removes any remaining impurities.

This is done through repeated washings and vaporizations. The Alchemist may add water or other substances to aid the distillation process.

Physical

The Alchemist takes the matter, adds water, and heats it on a steady flame until a vapor rises.

As the vapor comes back down, the Alchemist will collect it. This will purify the substance and further concentrate it.

The Distillation process will be done some number of times at the Alchemist's discretion. The matter will also be cleaned, if possible, after each distillation.

Anxiety Alchemist System

The Anxiety Alchemist will distill the new substance created during fermentation using a visualized dry run process.

By the end of the Distillation process, the alchemist will purify, refine, and concentrate the goodness contained within its new vessel.

Step 1 - The alchemist will visualize the steps experienced during the anxiety.

For example, a person who has anxiety about going to the movies will visualize the process: leaving the house, getting in the car, picking up a friend, driving to the theater, buying tickets and snacks, finding seats, watching the movie, dropping the friend off, driving home, and going inside.

Step 2 - The Alchemist will note all glitches (impurities along the way), such as an aspect of the original anxiety creeping in.

Step 3 - Next, any glitches noted will be written down on scraps of paper and then ceremoniously burned, as in the Calcination operation.

Step 4 - Repeat Steps 1 to 3 at least three times to complete the Anxiety Alchemy Distillation process.

<u>Example</u>

Step 1 - Erin gets comfortable on her couch, closes her eyes, and visualizes a commute to work.

This looks like:

- Get up for work and get ready for the new day.

- Drive to the train station and find parking in the closest lot.

- Go up to the train platform and stand in front of where the doors of her favorite car will open.

- Enter the car and get a good aisle seat.

- Larry introduces me to a few of his friends.

- The train arrives on time.

- Walk through Penn Station to the Subway.

- The subway is running on time.

- Get a seat on the Subway.

- Arrive at work early enough to grab a coffee at my favorite coffee shop.

- Have a great and productive day at work.

- Go out for drinks with coworkers after work.

- Get to socialize with people who never had the opportunity to meet the true me.

- Take the train home.

Step 2 - Erin notes the glitch she encounters. Some scary-looking dudes are by the Subway entrance, which makes her feel unsafe.

Step 3 - Erin then writes down "scary-looking dudes in the subway" on a scrap of paper and ceremoniously burns it.

Step 4 - Erin is very fortunate and does not experience any new glitches the second and third time distilling. Also, the scary-looking dudes glitch has been resolved.

To be sure, Erin decides to distill a couple more times to be entirely certain. But no other glitches are encountered.

Erin now feels that her vessel and its contents are completely refined and purified of any anxiety.

Chapter Twelve

Coagulation

The seventh and last operation of alchemy is Coagulation.

Coagulation is the solidification, or bringing together, of all parts to create the Philosopher's Stone.

Physical

The Alchemist will remove all traces of water in the created new matter.

They would have the Philosopher's Stone - Gold if they were successful.

Anxiety Alchemist System

Step 1 - There is only one way for the Anxiety Alchemist to undertake the Coagulation operation. One way to bring it all together.

That one way is to TEST.

In real life, go through the process where the anxiety to be alchemized is experienced.

How did the Alchemist do? Hopefully, they will experience the same positive results as my testing.

If the anxiety persists after live testing, the Alchemist may repeat the Anxiety Alchemy System from the start.

This is the only case where the AAS should be repeated for a particular anxiety.

Example

Step 1 - Erin sets off for a live test of her commute to work.

She notes that it is markedly better and that very little anxiety is experienced!

Erin feels that the little anxiety can be worked through with continued meditation and affirmations. So, there is no need to repeat the Anxiety Alchemy System for this particular anxiety.

Bonus Step: Erin is so happy with her results and absolutely loves the Anxiety Alchemy System. The only logical thing she can do is contact Mike, the Anxiety Alchemy Guy, and tell him of her positive experience.

Chapter 13

Anxiety Alchemy System Summary

I thought it would be helpful to include a summary of the Anxiety Alchemy System in one chapter as a form of a checklist.

Calcination

Step 1 - It is time to let your anxiety-caused emotions out in a controlled way. Get comfortable in your favorite meditation position. Be sure that you have paper and a writing implement nearby.

Step 2—We start calcination by heating ourselves mentally. Remember, Calcination requires extreme heat, so we are, in effect, preheating the oven. Use the "Bellows Breath" Meditation to do this.

Step 3—Now that we are warmed up, it is time to unleash our anxiety-related emotions. Do the "Roasting Cinnabar" meditation.

Step 4 - Now, the Anxiety Alchemist will symbolically calcinate the anxiety's component parts by burning them to ash.

Dissolution

Step 1 - It is now time for the Anxiety Alchemist to dissolve the white powder of their anxiety in water. What remains will likely be the components of their anxiety, both good and bad. Their burnt thoughts and emotions will dissolve into the water and no longer be a factor in their alchemical process.

Step 2 - Perform the "Bain Marie" meditation.

Separation

Step 1 - There are a bunch of harmful anxiety component materials in the alchemical solution.

The Anxiety Alchemist needs to sift those out. **They are done fueling this anxiety.** They have been burnt to ashes, drowned, and had all emotions disconnected from them.

If you remember, these are the components from Chapter Six—Calcination—the ones I requested the Alchemist duplicate.

Step 2 - Now, you are going to take the harmful components of the anxiety and symbolically drown them. The Alchemist may do this however they like.

My favorite way is to flush them down the toilet. I get to drown them and also wave goodbye to them.

Step 3—Our Alchemist is not done separating. They look at the alchemical solution. There are bright and glowing things. These are the good things that their anxiety has been suppressing—the things that their anxiety took hostage.

Well, they are back and better than ever.

Pull the "good things" out of the alchemical solution by writing them on scraps of paper or similar material. Take your time with this. If given a chance, there is probably more good than expected.

The Anxiety Alchemist may wish to put a few of their favorites somewhere visible in a room they frequent. For example, I have mine on my desk, hanging off the bottom of my computer monitor.

Step 4 - Perform the "Alchemistic Aeration Meditation" a few times. Good on them if the Alchemist wishes to take up the challenge in the meditation.

Conjunction

Step 1 - The good parts of the Anxiety extracted in the Separation operation are reviewed for completeness and actual tangible value.

Step 2 - This is the most crucial step of Conjunction - the secret ingredient, the binding agent of all binding agents, must be added to the Anxiety Alchemist's mixture.

This is the time when the Anxiety Alchemist adds their emotions back.

Do you remember that the Alchemist removed all emotions from their anxiety work in Chapter Six, Calcination? Then, they worked on it during Dissolution and Separation in a straightforward, logical, and arms-length manner.

Well now, they add the emotions back into the mixture of only good anxiety-related material.

Step 3 (Optional) - The last step of this operation is to perform an Earth meditation. The Alchemical Operation of Conjunction corresponds with the Earth.

Fermentation

Step 1 - Commit the list of goodness inside the anxiety shell to memory.

Step 2 - This second step needs to be done daily for at least a week, but no longer than it takes the Anxiety Alchemist to rot away the anxiety shell fully.

Step 2A - Each day, speak out loud the goodness list three times. This should be done from memory. When The Anxiety Alchemist does so, they do it with deliberation and sincerity. When each item is said, the Alchemist should experience a shot of well-being.

Step 2B - During the Anxiety Alchemist's putrification period, they must be penalized for every time a thought of a negative aspect comes to mind.

The Alchemist will choose their penalty. This is just plain old behavior modification. It also helps the alchemist focus on not letting those thoughts creep in.

Step 3 - Now, the Anxiety Alchemist will add something to the process to help the putrified remains of their Lesser Stone ferment into their future Philosopher's Stone.

They will take their rotted material and integrate it back into themself.

How this is done is left to the discretion of the Anxiety Alchemist.

Recommended methods include:

- Meditating on the goodness that is now re-integrated into the person.

- Repeating an affirmation regarding the particular anxiety no longer being a part of the Anxiety Alchemist.

Distillation

Step 1 - The process in which the anxiety used to be experienced will be visualized by the alchemist.

Step 2 - The Alchemist will note all glitches (impurities along the way), such as an aspect of the original anxiety creeping in.

Step 3 - Next, any glitches noted will be written down on scraps of paper and then ceremoniously burned, as was done in the Calcination operation.

Step 4 - Repeat Steps 1 to 3 at least three times to complete the Anxiety Alchemy Distillation process.

Coagulation

Step 1 - In real life, go through the process where the anxiety to be alchemized is experienced.

How did the Alchemist do? Hopefully, they will experience the same positive results as my testing.

If the anxiety persists after live testing, the Alchemist may repeat the Anxiety Alchemy System from the start.

Chapter 14

Conclusion

I very much hope that you will find the **Anxiety Alchemy System** to be a great supplemental treatment for anxiety.

I endeavored to present the System in a way that allows Maximum Flexibility.

However, I have a solution if you want a detailed and structured approach to Anxiety Alchemy.

I call it the **Detailed Anxiety Alchemy Method (DAAM)**, which is how I implement the Anxiety Alchemy System.

Along with many other tutorials, insights, and valuable information, I will teach the **DAAM** way in the *"Mike Guarneri Letter."*

The Mike Guarneri Letter will be the best physical monthly newsletter about using ancient wisdom to treat mental health issues. Be sure to subscribe.

If you have any questions, concerns, or comments, please contact me at support@mikeguarneri.com.